ORNITHOMIMUS
AND OTHER FAST DINOSAURS

by Dougal Dixon

illustrated by
Steve Weston and **James Field**

PICTURE WINDOW BOOKS
Minneapolis, Minnesota

Picture Window Books
5115 Excelsior Boulevard
Suite 232
Minneapolis, MN 55416
877-845-8392
www.picturewindowbooks.com

Printed in the United States of America.

Library of Congress Cataloging-in-Publication Data
Dixon, Dougal.
Ornithomimus and other fast dinosaurs / by Dougal
Dixon ; illustrated by Steve Weston & James Field.
p. cm. – (Dinosaur find)
Includes bibliographical references and index.
ISBN 1-4048-1326-8
1. Dinosaurs—Speed—Juvenile literature.
2. Ornithomimus—Speed—Juvenile literature.
I. Weston, Steve, ill. II. Field, James, 1959- ill. III. Title.
QE861.5.D626 2006
567.9—dc22   2005023330

Acknowledgments
This book was produced for Picture Window Books by
Bender Richardson White, U.K.

Illustrations by James Field (cover and pages 4–5, 7,
13, 17, 21) and Steve Weston (pages 9, 11, 15, 19).
Diagrams by Stefan Chabluk.
All photographs copyright Digital Vision except
page 20 (Ariadne Van Zandbergen/Frank Lane
Picture Agency).

Consultant: John Stidworthy, Scientific Fellow of
the Zoological Society, London, and former
Lecturer in the Education Department, Natural
History Museum, London.

Reading Adviser: Susan Kesselring, M.A., Literacy
Educator, Rosemount-Apple Valley-Eagan
(Minnesota) School District

Types of dinosaurs
In this book, a red shape at the top of a left-hand page shows the animal was a meat-eater. A green shape shows it was a plant-eater.

Just how big—or small— were they?
Dinosaurs were many different sizes. We have compared their sizes to one of the following:

Chicken
2 feet (60 centimeters) tall
6 pounds (2.7 kilograms)

Adult person
6 feet (1.8 meters) tall
170 pounds (76.5 kg)

Elephant
10 feet (3 m) tall
12,000 pounds
(5,400 kg)

TABLE OF CONTENTS

WHAT'S INSIDE?

Dinosaurs lived between 230 and 65 million years ago. These dinosaurs were some of the fastest. Find out how they lived and what they have in common with today's animals.

THE FASTEST DINOSAURS

There were all kinds of fast-running dinosaurs millions of years ago. Some of the small plant-eating dinosaurs had to run fast to get away from the meat-eaters. The meat-eating dinosaurs then became even faster to try to catch them. *Dromaeosaurus* was probably the fastest runner. It could reach a speed of 50 miles (80 kilometers) per hour.

Plant-eating *Ornithomimus* and *Dromiceiomimus* lived on the open plains. Fast-running meat-eaters such as *Dromaeosaurus* hunted them.

Ornithomimus looked like an ostrich. It had a tiny body and a tiny head. It also had long legs and a long neck. *Ornithomimus* didn't have any teeth. It had a beak instead. It probably ate fruits and insects.

Long neck today

An ostrich has a long neck like *Ornithomimus* did. It can see enemies from a long distance.

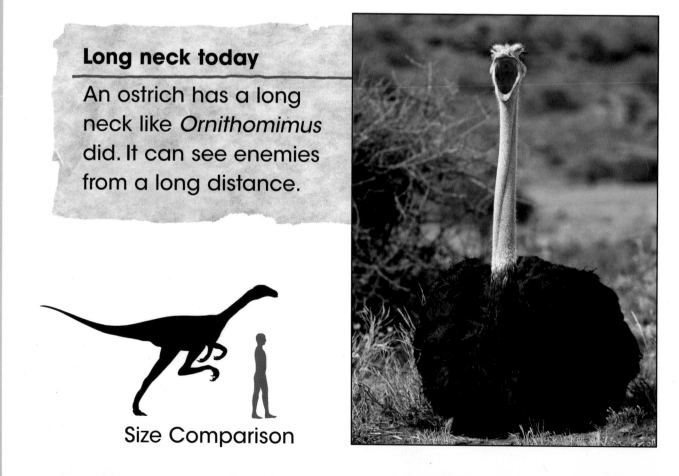

Size Comparison

With its small body and long legs, *Ornithomimus* could run as fast as a racehorse. Its long tail steadied this dinosaur as it ran.

PATAGONYKUS

Patagonykus was quite small. It could survive by just eating insects. It was too tiny to fight off its enemies. Instead, it would quickly run away on its long hind legs. It dug its long toes into the ground to give it an extra push forward.

Insect-eater today

Chimpanzees dig for insects, such as termites, like *Patagonykus* once did.

Size Comparison

Patagonykus had little arms, each with a single huge claw. It used these claws to scratch into the sides of termite nests to reach the insects.

Herds of plant-eating *Orodromeus* must have spent much of their time fleeing from packs of meat-eating *Troodon*. A newly hatched *Orodromeus* could run fast from the moment it left the egg.

Herd-runners today

Wildebeest run in herds like *Orodromeus* did. When a hunter comes near, the animals run in all directions. The hunter does not know which one to chase.

Size Comparison

Orodromeus had long legs that allowed it to run from one area of food to another. It also ran fast to escape from the meat-eaters.

DROMAEOSAURUS

Pronunciation:
DROH-mee-uh-SAW-rus

Dromaeosaurus could run faster than a greyhound. It had sharp claws on its toes. It used its claws for tearing into the flesh of the animals that it chased and killed.

Fast-runners today

Cheetahs run very fast, chase down animals, and use their teeth to kill prey like *Dromaeosaurus* did millions of years ago.

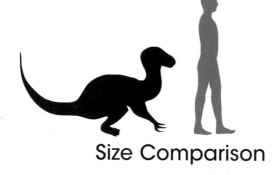

Size Comparison

Dromaeosaurus would catch its prey with the claws on its hands. Then it would tear the prey apart with its toe claws and many sharp teeth.

13

Saurornithoides had long legs, strong fingers, and large eyes. It had good eyesight. Sometimes it hunted at night. It chased after prey deep in the forests. It was fast enough to run down swift-footed animals like lizards.

Forest hunter today

The Florida panther has good eyesight and strong claws like *Saurornithoides* did. It also often hunts in forests at night.

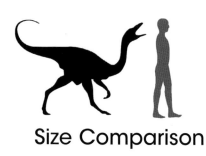

Size Comparison

Saurornithoides had big claws on its feet. It used the claws for catching and killing its prey. It picked up the animal with its hands and tore at the flesh with its sharp teeth.

Dromiceiomimus was just like *Ornithomimus* but much bigger. It had long fingers on its hands. It used its fingers to uncover food on the ground. When *Dromiceiomimus* ran, it tucked its arms into its body.

Long beak today

The saddle-billed stork bends its long neck and uses its long beak to pick up food like *Dromiceiomimus* did.

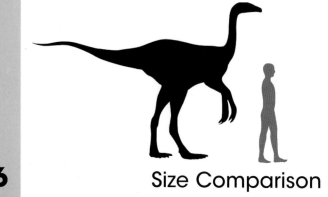

Size Comparison

When *Dromiceiomimus* raised its long neck and head, it could see for a long way. It could tell if any enemies were coming and get a head start.

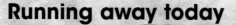

ZEPHYROSAURUS

Pronunciation:
ZEF-i-ruh-SAW-rus

Zephyrosaurus has a name that means "lizard of the wind." With its long hind legs, it must have run as fast as the wind. It needed to be fast to cross the open spaces to find food before being seen by other dinosaurs.

Running away today

Antelopes often feed beside streams as *Zephyrosaurus* did. When danger comes, they run away.

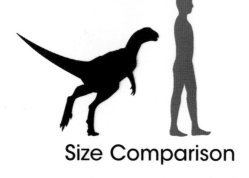

Size Comparison

Zephyrosaurus was a two-footed plant-eater like *Orodromeus*. It could not fight. It could not hide. Whenever there was danger, it just ran.

Avimimus looked like a bird when it ran. It lived in herds for protection. When a big meat-eating dinosaur attacked, it would not know which *Avimimus* to try to catch.

Moving together today

Desert animals like camels move about in groups like *Avimimus* did millions of years ago.

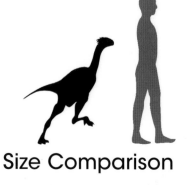

Size Comparison

The beak of an *Avimimus* was short. *Avimimus* ate the little insects that lived on the open plains at the end of the Age of Dinosaurs.

WHERE DID THEY GO?

Dinosaurs are extinct, which means that none of them are alive today. Scientists study rocks and fossils to find clues about what happened to dinosaurs.

People have different explanations about what happened. Some people think a huge asteroid hit Earth and caused all sorts of climate changes, which caused the dinosaurs to die. Others think volcanic eruptions caused the climate to change and that killed the dinosaurs. No one knows for sure what happened to all the dinosaurs.

GLOSSARY

beak—the hard front part of the mouth of birds and some dinosaurs

claws—tough, usually curved fingernails or toenails

hatch—to break out of an egg

herds—large groups of animals that move, feed, and sleep together

insects—small, six-legged animals; they include ants, bees, beetles, and flies

nest—home for an animal's eggs or babies

packs—groups of animals that hunt and kill together

plains—large areas of flat land with few large plants

prey—animals that are hunted by other animals for food

To Learn More

At the Library

Clark, Neil, and William Lindsay. *1001 Facts About Dinosaurs.* New York: Backpack Books, Dorling Kindersley, 2002.

Dixon, Dougal. *Dougal Dixon's Amazing Dinosaurs.* Honesdale, Penn.: Boyds Mills Press, 2000.

Holtz, Thomas, and Michael Brett-Surman. *Jurassic Park Institute Dinosaur Field Guide.* New York: Random House, 2001.

On the Web

FactHound offers a safe, fun way to find Web sites related to this book. All of the sites on FactHound have been researched by our staff.

1. Visit *www.facthound.com*

2. Type in this special code: 1404813268

3. Click on the FETCH IT button.

Your trusty FactHound will fetch the best sites for you!

Look for all of the books in the Dinosaur Find series:

Index